BULLETPROOF

WRITTEN AND ILLUSTRATED BY
KATE FISCHER

ISBN 978-1-7360598-0-7
PRINTED IN THE UNITED STATES OF AMERICA

www.littlefischbooks.com

For Charlie.
I pray that you always stand tall, proud, and strong.

I love you no matter what.
Mama

THIS BOOK BELONGS TO:

_____

Preface

I wrote this book for my son, Charlie. He loves fictional stories about good vs. evil. He loves building forts and wrestling. He loves adventures in the woods and using sticks as weapons in epic battles against imaginary bad guys. What I want kids like Charlie to know is that you really are warriors and our country needs you!

War is very real. People fight for power, money, or freedom. There always seems to be something to fight about. And behind the field of every battle someone has developed a strategy to fight against their enemy. To win in combat, you've got to have the right plan and resources. Unfortunately, very few of us know how to fight the right way. In fact, most of the time we don't even understand who we're really fighting against.

There's a book in the Bible called Ephesians. It is basically a letter written by the apostle Paul to teach Christians how to protect themselves against the evil plans of the devil. He explained that when fighting against evil spirits, we are protected by the full armor of God. We call this type of warfare a spiritual battle. It's important that we acknowledge the reality of evil in our culture. I mean, how can we defeat an enemy if we don't even admit that he exists? I know it sounds crazy but the devil really is alive and active in our world today. Just as he was when Paul wrote that letter thousands of years ago.

As Christians, we are empowered by the Holy Spirit to battle against the evil forces of this world and while doing so we are protected by an army of angels and the whole armor of God. This doesn't mean we should go physically attack everyone who doesn't share our values. Nor does it mean we are immune to physical injury. It means we need to be awake to the destructive forces influencing us and through intentional prayer, we go to war. It means being brave enough to tell others about God to help build his army. It means your faith will shield you when satan attacks your thoughts. It means trusting in God's plan above all else.

Ephesians 6: 10-17

10 Last of all I want to remind you that your strength must come from the Lord's mighty power within you. 11 Put on all of God's armor so that you will be able to stand safe against all strategies and tricks of Satan. 12 For we are not fighting against people made of flesh and blood, but against persons without bodies—the evil rulers of the unseen world, those mighty satanic beings and great evil princes of darkness who rule this world; and against huge numbers of wicked spirits in the spirit world.

13 So use every piece of God's armor to resist the enemy whenever he attacks, and when it is all over, you will still be standing up.

14 But to do this, you will need the strong belt of truth and the breastplate of God's approval. 15 Wear shoes that are able to speed you on as you preach the Good News of peace with God. 16 In every battle you will need faith as your shield to stop the fiery arrows aimed at you by Satan. 17 And you will need the helmet of salvation and the sword of the Spirit—which is the Word of God.

There are battles we face
As we walk through each day.

Some while we work
And some while we play.

Some battles are big.
Some battles are small.

But we have a Leader
Who will conquer them all.

A big storm is coming.
You must fight in this war.

A spiritual battle
Like never before.

Don't feel afraid
As you enter this fight.

For you are protected
By angels in flight.

To prepare for this conflict
A fort must be made.

Create your own war room
To worship and pray.

Gear up for battle
From your head to your toes.

And God's love will shield you
Like bulletproof clothes.

The helmet protects the thoughts in your mind,
Blocking out evil to help you be kind.

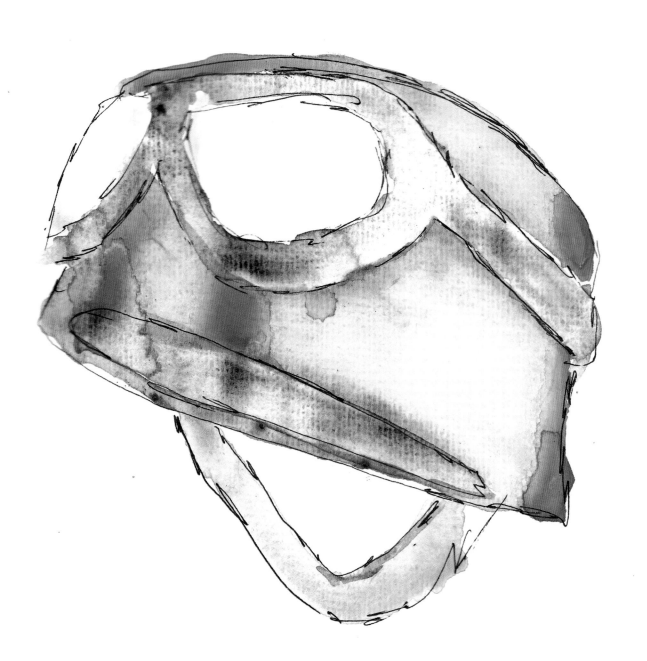

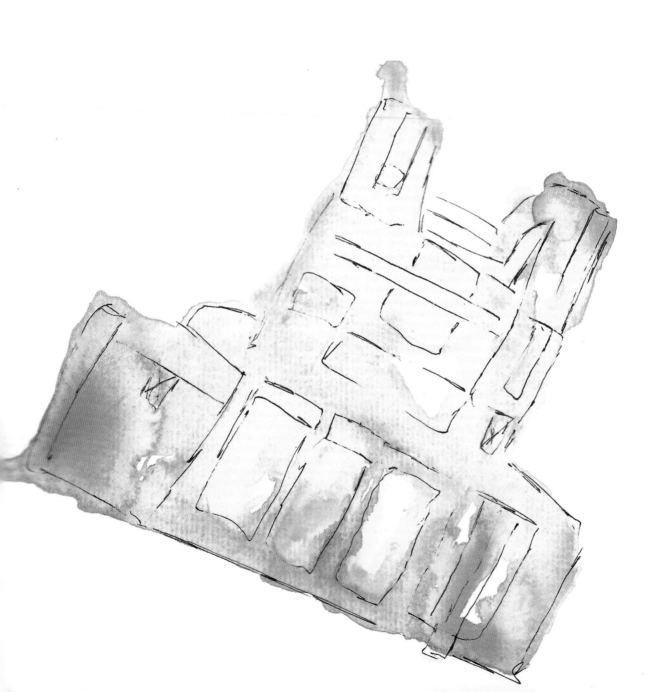

A thick piece of armor
Is strapped to your chest
To safeguard your heart
When you're put to the test.

Flaming arrows will fly
in the dark of the night.

But your shield will protect
And your light will shine bright.

FOR GOD GAVE US A SPIRIT
NOT OF FEAR BUT OF
POWER AND LOVE AND SELF-CONTROL.
2 TIMOTHY 1:6-7

**With knowledge is power
And it sharpens your sword.**

**To strike down all evil
With words of the Lord.**

Last but not least
Are the boots on your feet.

To travel the world
And tell all that you meet.

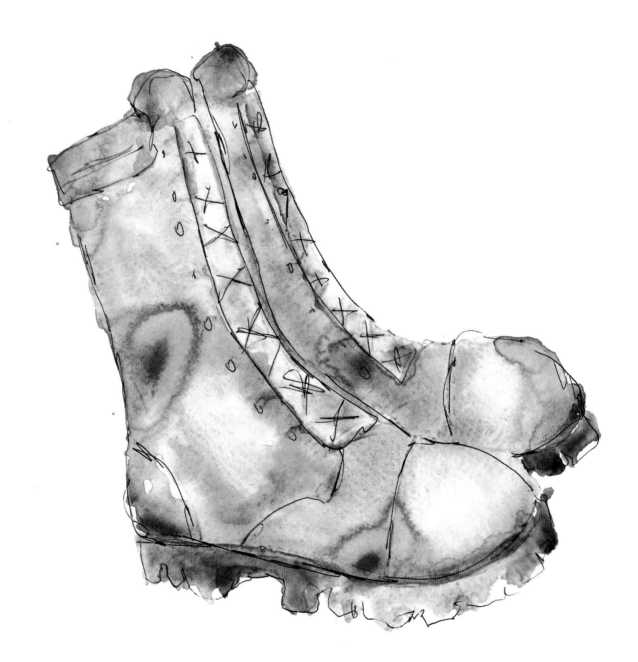

Very truly I tell you,
You're never alone.

The Lord God Almighty
Has called you His own.

Look up to the sky
When you're under attack.

There are soldiers in heaven,
And they've all got your back.

Our country feels broken;
Full of hatred and sin.

But be brave and courageous.
WITH GOD YOU WILL WIN!

About the Author

Once upon a time, Kate Fischer was a rebellious teenager. Today she loves coffee, Jesus, and America too. She is the author and illustrator of *Sunshine* and the #1 best seller *Your Angel Army*. Kate holds a B.F.A. from St. Cloud State University and is the owner of Little Fisch Design and Little Fisch Books. She is passionate about supporting small businesses and has a deep respect for those serving in the military.

When she's not painting or writing, you can probably find her out in the woods with her country-boy husband and their 3 splendid children.